MAJOR
World Cities

SYDNEY

Mason Crest
450 Parkway Drive, Suite D
Broomall, PA 19008
www.masoncrest.com
Developed and produced by Mason Crest

Printed and bound in the United States of America.

First printing
9 8 7 6 5 4 3 2 1

Series ISBN: 978-1-4222-3538-6
ISBN: 978-1-4222-3546-1
ebook ISBN: 978-1-4222-8366-0

Library of Congress Cataloging-in-Publication Data is on file with the publisher.

Picture credits

Cover: Salkit Leung/Dreamstime. Associated Press Picture Library : 41tl. Australian Picture Library: 30, /Barbara Zussine 13, /Charbaux 27, /Craig Lamotte 12b, 42, /D & Heaton 15tr, /Dave Morgan 28tl, /David Ball 34tr, /Eric Sierins 31tr, /Esther Beaton 35tl, /Flying Photos 37tr, /J. Carnemolla 4, 5b, 12t, 22tl, 23t, 26b, 29tl, 38b, 38t, 39t, 39b, /Jonathan Marks 16t, 18, 21cr, /JP & ES Baker 17bl, /Nick Rains 15bl, /Oliver Strewe 15tl, 36tr, /Peter Brennan 5t, / R. Garvey 11b, /Steve Vidler 19bl, /Strawberry Col. 23b. Coo-ee Historical Picture Library: 8, 9b, 9t, 10b, l0t, 11t, 26t, 40tr. Dreamstime.com: Gigsy222 11 br, Chris Howey 16tr, Ruzalmy 22 br, Moanakub 24 tr, Featureflash 25t, Pominoz 24-25b, Tuayai 28 r, Laurence Agron 41 br; Newscom/UPI/John Angelillo 24 tr; Robert Harding Picture Library: 14, 19tr, 20t, 24, 28br, 33bl, 34bl, 36bl. PopSugar.au: 43 br. Hogarth Galleries Pty. Ltd., Aboriginal Art Centers: 35br. Art Gallery of New South Wales, Mollie Gowing Acquisition Fund for Contemporary Aboriginal Art 1996 /© courtesy Anthony Wallis, Aboriginal Artists Agency Ltd., Sydney: CLIFFORD POSSUM TJAPALTJARRI, Lungkata's two sons at Warlugulong, 1976, synthetic polymer paint on canvas board, 70.5 x 55.0 cm: 33tr. N.H.P.A. /A.N.T: 16b, 17tr. Rex Features: 21tl, 29cr, 37bl, 40bl, 43tl. WildlightPhoto Agency: /Andrew Rankin 22cr, /Philip Quirk 20bl, 31bl, 32.

Words in **bold** are explained in the glossary on pages 46 and 47.

MAJOR
World Cities

BEIJING

BERLIN

LONDON

MOSCOW

NEW YORK

PARIS

ROME

SYDNEY

CONTENTS

INTRODUCTION

The city of Sydney lies on the Southeastern coast of Australia, on either side of a spectacular harbor that leads into the brilliant blue waters of the Pacific Ocean. Sydney is Australia's largest and oldest city, founded in 1788. Its central area covers just over 2.3 sq miles (6 sq km). Suburbs sprawl to the north, south and west to give Sydney a total area of about 4.8 sq miles (12.4 sq km). About 4.4 million people, known as Sydneysiders, live within its borders.

Pacific port

Sydney has become a major port for both passenger and cargo ships. Many luxury liners moor at Darling Harbor and Circular Quay, in the main Sydney Harbor area. Most **container ships**, which carry goods to and from places all over the world, dock further south, in Botany Bay. Sydney is also the most important base of the Royal Australian Navy. Its ships cluster around the navy headquarters on Garden Island.

Early settlers ▲ were stunned by the beauty of Sydney's harbor. Today, with its many tall buildings and its famous bridge, it is still breathtaking.

SYDNEY

STATUS

Capital of **state** of New South Wales (NSW)

AREA

4.8 sq miles (12.4 square km)

POPULATION

4,400,000 (2014)

GOVERNING BODY

State government and local councils, including the City Council of Sydney

CLIMATE

Temperatures average 78°F (26°C) in February and 60°F (16°C) in July

TIME ZONE

Greenwich Mean Time plus 10 hours

CURRENCY

1 Australian dollar (A$) = 100 cents

OFFICIAL LANGUAGE

English

Leisurely lifestyle

Sydney's location has helped to create the city's special way of life. Many Sydneysiders regularly visit the harbor beaches, as well as the 37 miles (60 km) of Pacific coastline. Swimming, surfing, sailing, and other water sports are all popular and people spend many hours outside. Sydney's climate makes this outdoor lifestyle possible. Summers (December to February) are warm and sunny, while winters (June to August) are usually mild. But there are occasional downpours, and sometimes a strong summer wind, the Southerly Buster, blows through the city.

A container ship waits in the terminal at ▲ Botany Bay. Cargo is packed into straightsided containers like those on the deck.

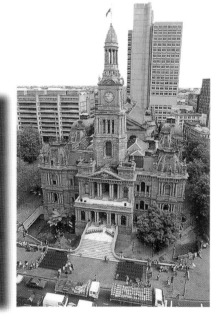

The City Council ➤ of Sydney meets in Sydney Town Hall. It is one of many local councils in the city and controls only about 2.3 sq miles (6 sq km) of land.

State capital

Sydney is the capital of New South Wales, one of Australia's six states. The state parliament meets in the city. It controls some aspects of Sydney life, such as schools and railways. Local councils and other special organizations look after matters such as parks, roads, and libraries.

MAPS OF THE CITY

These maps show you Sydney as it is today. The area map shows Sydney's vast suburbs and Pacific beaches, and the street map gives a closer view of the city center. Many of the places mentioned in the book are marked.

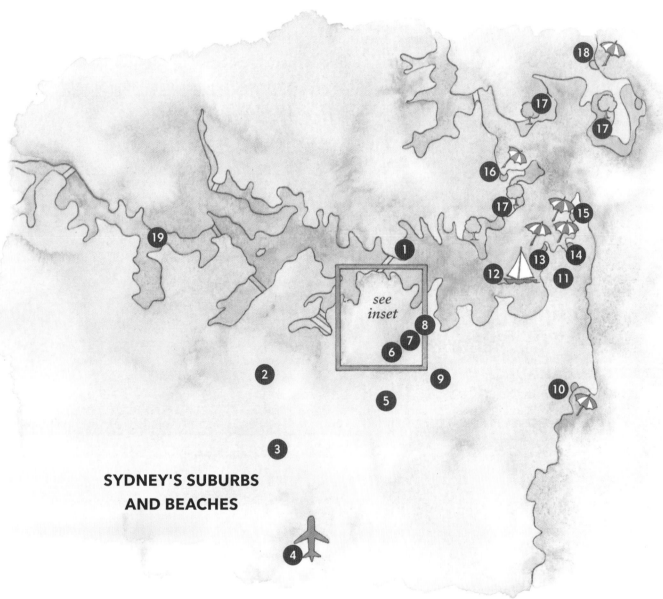

SYDNEY'S SUBURBS AND BEACHES

1. Kirribilli
2. Leichhardt
3. Marrickville
4. Kingsford Smith Airport
5. Redfern
6. Surry Hills
7. Darlinghurst
8. Kings Cross
9. Paddington
10. Bondi Beach
11. Vaucluse
12. Sydney Harbor (Port Jackson)
13. Shark Bay
14. Parsley Bay
15. Watsons Bay
16. Balmoral
17. Sydney Harbor National Park
18. Manly
19. Parramatta River

1	Powerhouse Museum
2	Chinatown
3	Chinese Garden
4	Darling Harbor
5	Sydney Town Hall
6	Queen Victoria Building
7	State Theatre
8	Great Synagogue
9	Anzac Memorial
10	Australian Museum
11	St Mary's Cathedral
12	Hyde Park
13	Sydney Tower
14	St James' Church
15	Hyde Park Barracks
16	Art Gallery of NSW
17	The Domain
18	State Parliament House
19	Museum of Sydney
20	Royal Botanic Gardens
21	Justice and Police Museum
22	Circular Quay
23	Museum of Contemporary Art
24	Sydney Observatory
25	Cadman's Cottage
26	Central Business District
27	Sydney Opera House
28	Sydney Harbor Tunnel
29	Sydney Harbor Bridge

CENTRAL SYDNEY

SYDNEY'S EARLY HISTORY

Australia's first inhabitants were the Aborigines, who arrived from Southeast Asia at least 40,000 years ago. Aboriginal tribes gradually spread south and about 20,000 years later had reached the area that is now Sydney Harbor. The main Aboriginal tribe there was the Eora. Its members lived in caves or bark huts. They ate mostly fish and shellfish, but also hunted animals and gathered plants, birds' eggs, and honey.

Captain Phillip raised the Union Jack ➤ at Sydney Cove on 26 January 1788. This is an early 20th-century painting of the flag-raising scene.

Captain Cook

The Aborigines probably met no one from outside Australia for thousands of years. Then, on 29 April 1770, English explorer Captain James Cook and his crew landed in Botany Bay, 10 miles (16 km) south of Sydney Harbor. The Aborigines threw spears at the strangers, then ran off into the bush. The Europeans studied the bay before making their way up Australia's east coast, which they claimed for Britain and named New South Wales.

Penal colony

In 1786 the British government decided to set up a **penal colony** in Botany Bay. On 13 May 1787 the First Fleet of 11 ships set sail for Australia. On board were its leader, Captain Arthur Phillip, more than 700 soldiers and sailors with their families, and 736 convicts. The fleet arrived in January 1788, but the bay's poor soil and lack of fresh water made it unsuitable for settlement. So Captain Phillip sailed north and found a better harbor—Sydney Cove.

A hard life

Conditions in the penal colony were harsh. Convicts toiled under the hot sun to build huts, first from wood and mud, then from brick. They also planted crops, but these did not grow well. The newcomers almost starved before the Second Fleet arrived with food in 1790. Meanwhile, relations between Europeans and Aborigines grew more hostile.

▼ A small group of Aborigines (bottom left) looks on as the Sydney settlement grows. This picture dates from 1802.

The making of a city

The settlement slowly grew. It soon contained not only convicts but also free settlers, who began to arrive in 1793. Then, in 1810, a dynamic Scot called Lachlan Macquarie became Governor of New South Wales. He worked with the convict architect Francis Greenway (see page 40) to construct roads and public buildings. By the end of his 11-year rule, Sydney was a true city. In 1813 explorers crossed the Blue Mountains west of Sydney and discovered vast grasslands. Soon thousands more free settlers arrived to set up sheep farms there, and wool became a major export.

Governor Lachlan Macquarie was an ▲ army officer who had worked in both India and the Middle East before setting out for Sydney with his wife.

A new era

By 1840 about 83,000 convicts had been shipped to Sydney. About 70,000 free settlers had also made their way to the city. In that year the British stopped sending criminals to New South Wales, and a new era in the city's life began.

Sydney was officially declared a city in 1842 when it had a population of about 60,000. Then, in 1851, gold was discovered west of the Blue Mountains. **Prospectors** rushed to the region, and by 1890 about 400,000 people lived in the city.

◄ Men pan for gold in the Ophir Goldfields west of Sydney. Many thousands went to the site in the 1850s, but few made their fortunes.

Trading wealth

Population growth and trade in wool and wheat turned Sydney into a wealthy community. Men paved the city's dusty streets with wood and constructed solid buildings that showed its new status. Among them were the Customs House (1887) and the Town Hall (1889).

Political change

In 1855 Sydney politicians set up a parliament, and in 1856 the city became capital of the New South Wales colony. In 1901, New South Wales joined five other colonies to form Australia and became a **state** of this new nation. Sydney became the state capital.

Poverty and crime

There was poverty too. Many people lived in slums, especially in the Rocks district near the harbor, where gangs of thieves roamed. In 1900 rats spread plague through the city, and 112 people died. The rats were killed and the slums cleared to prevent further outbreaks.

World War I

Many Sydney citizens fought in the **World War I** (1914-18), most famously at Gallipoli in Turkey. The Anzac Memorial in Sydney's Hyde Park commemorates them. After the war, in the early 1930s, economic **depression** struck Sydney. Unemployment soared, but the wool trade recovered and new industries grew.

World War II

Sydneysiders also fought in the **World War II** (1939-45), both overseas and at home. On 31 May 1942 three Japanese submarines sailed into Sydney Harbor to attack an American ship. They did not reach their target and were sunk.

Immigration and expansion

After the war, in 1947, the Australian government encouraged immigration to provide skilled workers for industry. Thousands of people from many countries poured into Sydney. The city has continued to grow ever since. In 2013 Sydney celebrated its 225th anniversary.

◀ The Sydney of 1802 is no longer recognizable in this 1905 photo. In 100 years, the settlement had become an impressive city.

Australian soldiers in the trenches at ▼ Gallipoli, where they fought from 1915-16. The ill-planned attack cost 36,000 lives.

BIG CELEBRATIONS

When Sydney celebrated its first centenary (100th birthday) in 1888, there were joyful street parades and a **regatta** in the harbor. A new park, Centennial Park, was opened. Thirteen years later, the ceremony to mark the birth of Australia was held there. When Sydney reached 200 in 1988, the festivities were even more magnificent. The Summer Olympics drew the attention of the world to Sydney in 2000, with Sydney Harbor the centerpiece of the opening and closing celebrations. In 2015, the nation remembered the 100th anniversary of the events at Gallipoli (above).

Most of the early settlers in Sydney were British or Irish. By the end of World War II, these two groups still formed about 95 per cent of the population. But the immigration policy introduced by the government after the war has transformed Sydney into a truly multicultural city.

New arrivals

The first postwar immigrants to arrive were from Europe, especially Greece, Italy, Turkey, and Yugoslavia. Members of each nationality stayed together and set up communities. Many Greeks, for example, settled in the suburb of Marrickville.

Football fans in the suburb ▲ of Leichhardt show their support for the Italian team in the 2014 World Cup of soccer.

Different peoples

At first, the national government encouraged only white Europeans to come to Australia, but in the 1960s Asian people began to arrive. In 1976 many Lebanese people came to Sydney, escaping from civil war at home. Refugees from war in Vietnam and Cambodia soon followed. In the 1990s, large numbers of Hong Kong Chinese also arrived. In the 2010s, the largest numbers of immigrants come from India, China, New Zealand, and the UK.

◄ This ornate gateway marks the entrance to Dixon Street, an area in the Chinatown district of Sydney.

Religious life

Most early Sydneysiders were Christians: either British Protestants or Irish Roman Catholics. By the late 19th century there were two cathedrals in the city, St. Andrew's for **Anglican** worshippers and St. Mary's for Catholics. Today the city contains many other Christian groups, too, including a large Greek Orthodox community. About 30,000 Jews live in modern Sydney and worship in the Great Synagogue. There are thousands of Muslims in the city too, many of whose families came from Indonesia, Turkey, and Lebanon.

Harmony and racism

The Australian government promotes racial harmony and in 1989 published its *National Agenda for a Multicultural Australia*. Relations between Aborigines and whites are better, but still a work in progress. In 2003, Linda Burney of the Australian Labor Party became the first indigenous person elected to the New South Wales Parliament (2003). In 2008, the government issued a formal apology to native peoples for past treatment.

THE ABORIGINES

Fifty years after the first convicts arrived in Sydney, almost all the Iora Aborigines (see pages 8-9) had died. Many were killed by European diseases such as cholera, to which they had no immunity. Other Aborigines moved into the city, but the settlers destroyed their way of life, took their land and forced them to live on **reservations**. Today Aborigines make up only 1.2 per cent of Sydney's population. Many of them live in the suburbs of Redfern and La Perouse. Many have poor housing and little money. But a strong Aboriginal rights movement has emerged. A national movement known as "Recognize" encourages the ongoing dialogue to remove racism from public life.

This Sea of Hands display (above) was put up on Bondi Beach in 1998 to draw attention to Aborigines' claims for justice.

BUILDINGS AND BRIDGES

Sydney's two world-famous landmarks—Sydney Harbor Bridge and Sydney Opera House—make the city instantly recognizable. But a trip through the streets reveals many other impressive buildings.

Spotlights pick out Sydney ▼ Opera House and Sydney Harbor Bridge at night, creating a spectacular scene.

Sydney Harbor Bridge

In Sydney's early years, the only way to cross from the north to the south shore of the city was to take a ferry across the water. Then, in 1932, Sydney Harbor Bridge opened. Its magnificent arch is 550 yards (503 m) long and contains more than 50,000 tons of steel. Sydneysiders call it the Coat Hanger because of its shape. The bridge carries eight lanes of traffic, two railway lines, a cycle track, and a footpath. A popular guided tour now lets visitors climb to the top for an amazing view.

The Opera House

In 1955 the Sydney authorities decided to build a new concert hall. They organized an international competition for architects. The winning plan was the spectacular shell design of Danish architect Jørn Utzon. There were many difficulties during construction, but Sydney Opera House was eventually opened by Queen Elizabeth II in 1973. The magnificent structure, which stands on Bennelong Point at the very edge of the harbor, contains not only an opera theatre, but also three other concert halls, restaurants, and bars.

◄ Visitors to the Hyde Park Barracks museum can sleep in hammocks there overnight, just as convicts once did.

The thin column of Sydney ► Tower is held firmly in place by 56 massive steel cables.

Macquarie Street

Macquarie Street was a dirt track until Lachlan Macquarie (see pages 8-9) turned it into an elegant road. Its fine buildings include the Hyde Park Barracks (1819). This once housed 600 convicts but now contains a museum of convict life. The city's oldest church, St. James' Church (1820), is also on the street. The copper on its roof was marked with arrows so that if convicts stole it, the metal could be identified and returned. Here, too, are State Parliament House, where people can watch political debates, and the State Library of New South Wales.

THE ROCKS

The harborside Rocks area, so called because of its rocky shoreline, was where Sydney's first settlers lived. Since the 1970s many of its old buildings have been restored. Now it attracts tourists eager to learn about the city's origins. Among the sights is Cadman's Cottage (below). It was built in 1816 and is the

oldest surviving building in central Sydney. Nearby Sydney Observatory (1858) was where astronomers used to study the heavens. Today it is a popular astronomy museum.

Sydney Tower

Sydney Tower was completed in 1981. It is 1,000 feet (305 m) tall, the highest building in the city. The view from the observation platform at the top is truly breathtaking. Visitors can see the harbor area, Botany Bay to the south and sometimes the Blue Mountains, far to the west.

PARKS AND GARDENS

Sydney has many large parks where people can relax and shelter from the heat under shady trees. The city is also surrounded by huge national parks, whose land and wildlife is protected by the **state**.

The Royal Botanic Gardens

The 75-acre (30-hectare) Royal Botanic Gardens overlook Sydney Harbor. This is where convicts grew vegetables on Australia's first farm. Today the gardens contain plants such as fig and eucalyptus trees. Special sites in the park include the Calyx, which scheduled to open in June 2016, as part of the garden's bicentenary celebration. The Calyx will present unique horticultural, botanical, and cultural exhibitions.

▲ The Royal Botanic Gardens were founded in 1856, and continue to grow and change, just like the plants!

NATIONAL PARKS

Sydney has ten national parks. Sydney Harbor National Park is made up of seven separate harborside locations, as well as Clark, Shark, and Rodd Islands. The other parks are far away from the city. The largest is the Royal National Park, to the south. It is mainly heathland, but also contains forests and sandy beaches. Ku-ring-gai Chase National Park, to the north, is the place to see Aboriginal rock art. Walkers have to watch out for poisonous spiders such as the Redback (right).

Plants from both ➤ China and Australia surround the pavilion in Sydney's Chinese Garden. They are intended to be living signs of the two countries' friendship.

The Domain

The Domain is a park next to the Botanic Gardens. Here people can visit the Andrew 'Boy' Charlton swimming pool and the Art Gallery of New South Wales. The Domain hosts open-air classical concerts in January, the middle of Australia's summer. People come to the park on Sundays to express their views. Crowds gather to listen—and to shout back if they disagree. This tradition began in the late 19th century and since then there have been some eccentric speakers, for example a man who dressed as an ancient Roman.

Taronga Zoo runs programs to breed endangered species such as red pandas (below) and snow leopards. ▼

Taronga Zoo

Taronga Zoo was set up on Sydney's north shore in 1916. Today its 75 acres (30 hectares) house more than 4,000 animals. Many of these, such as koalas and wombats, live only in Australia. Moats rather than cages are used to keep people and dangerous animals apart. There are also opportunities to get close to the zoo's friendlier creatures. On the Australian Walkabout tour, visitors can wander among wallabies and kangaroos.

The Chinese Garden of Friendship

Sydney is a sister city with Guangzhou, China. Landscape architects from this city designed the Chinese Garden of Friendship, in Darling Harbor. The garden contains many Chinese features, including jasmine bushes, weeping willow trees, a **pavilion,** and a lake filled with koi carp. Visitors can drink Chinese tea and eat dim sum in the garden teahouse.

BAYS AND BEACHES

The uneven coastline of Sydney Harbor has hundreds of beautiful bays with long beaches of yellow and white sand. Sydneysiders head for the beaches at every opportunity—not only at weekends, but also after a long day in the factory or office. They go to swim, sail or simply to enjoy the sunshine and the view.

▲ A few bathers wade into the tranquil water of Watsons Bay. The golden beaches around Sydney Harbor attract visitors from around the world.

Harbor beaches

One of the most famous harbor beaches is Watsons Bay, on the south shore. It was once a small fishing village, but has now become a favorite spot for family picnics and seafood restaurants. Some of the most popular beaches are Parsley Bay and Shark Bay, in the wealthy area of Vaucluse. One of the best beaches on the north shore is Balmoral, where the swimming is safe for children, and fish and chip shops line the waterfront. The waves are not large enough for surfing anywhere in the harbor, which is why many Sydneysiders make their way to the Pacific Ocean.

BEACH SAFETY

There are drawbacks to Sydney's seaside lifestyle. The ocean's powerful currents can be deadly, so trained lifeguards patrol many beaches. They use flags to mark areas where it is safe to swim and keep a lookout for anyone in trouble. They also watch out for sharks, which occasionally attack ocean swimmers or make their way into the harbor. For this reason, many harbor bays contain protected swimming areas that are enclosed by shark nets.

▼ The popularity of Bondi Beach often leads to overcrowding, as well as litter on the sand and in the streets nearby.

Bondi Beach

The Pacific beach closest to central Sydney is the world-famous Bondi Beach, to the south. Its towering breakers and half-mile expanse of soft sand attract surfers from all over the world, as well as swimmers and sunbathers.

▼ Manly's main pedestrian area, The Corso, contains many shops and restaurants, as well as a street market at weekends.

Surfing paradise

The most famous surfing beach on the Pacific coast north of Sydney was named Manly by Captain Arthur Phillip after the Aborigines who lived there were just that. Today Manly is a very popular resorts. Visitors enjoy whale watching, paddle boarding, and snorkeling, or the Manly Sea Life Sanctuary and Waterworks.

HOMES AND HOUSING

In the early 19th century, the main part of Sydney was around the harbor. But the city quickly spread, especially after the gold rush of the 1850s (see pages 10-11). Most settlers wanted to build a house of their own, so they added suburb after suburb to the city. As a result, Sydney expanded south, north and west, then along the Pacific coast. Now the city has about 650 suburbs.

Paddington houses ▲ such as these, with their delicate ironwork balconies, are protected by the Australian National Trust.

Paddington

Paddington, popularly known as Paddo, is one of Sydney's most famous inner suburbs. It is east of the center and contains rows of 19th-century terraced houses. Many have balconies made of 'Sydney lace' ironwork, featuring designs of Australian plants and animals. Paddington was once a poor area, but is now fashionable.

OUTER SUBURBS

Most Sydneysiders do not live in the terraces and flats of the inner suburbs. Instead, they inhabit sprawling outer suburbs such as Sylvania Waters in the southwest (left). Here the most common homes are cement- or brick-walled bungalows with red-tiled roofs. Many have a garden, a garage, and a swimming pool attached. Some people complain that the outer suburbs are all the same and have no character. But they provide decent, affordable housing for many thousands of Sydneysiders.

▲ Aboriginal paintings cover the side of a house in this Redfern street. The poverty of these surroundings is clear to see.

Redfern

The inner suburb of Redfern lies south of the city center. Many Aborigines who came to Sydney from other parts of Australia settled there and created their own style of housing. They painted the outsides of existing terraced houses in the reds and browns of traditional Aboriginal art. They also knocked down walls inside to make large rooms where **extended families** could live together. Redfern is changing as developers renovate houses and sell them at high prices.

Kirribilli

The small suburb of Kirribilli, on Sydney's north shore, is the most densely populated in the city. Like other inner suburbs, it contains many high-rise blocks divided into apartments, known as home units. It also has many luxurious harborside mansions owned by wealthy people. Kirribilli House, the Australian Prime Minister's Sydney home, and Admiralty House, where Australia's **Governor-General** lives, are also in Kirribilli.

Sydney Harbor Bridge can be glimpsed ▲ behind the tower blocks of Kirribilli in this waterside scene.

Federation Style

When Australia was founded in 1901, its six **states** joined in a **federation**. Soon afterwards, many Sydney homes were built in the new Federation Style of architecture. Features of the style include tiled roofs, **gables**, verandas and stained-glass windows. The southern suburb of Haberfield is filled with bungalows of this type, which is why it is known as the Federation Suburb.

EDUCATION

In Australia every **state** provides children with both primary and secondary education. Children in New South Wales must attend school from age six to fifteen. Some children start preschool education at three and many continue their education until they are sixteen or eighteen. Most pupils go to government-funded schools, but in Sydney there are also private schools. Pupils in both types of school usually wear a uniform.

▲ A group of Sydney primary school children. Some of the boys are wearing caps to protect their necks from the sun.

Curriculum choices

The Australian curriculum has eight key areas of learning: English; mathematics; science; humanities and social sciences; the arts; technologies; health and physical education; and languages.

Australian schoolchildren ▲ learn how to use computers at an early age.

Languages

Language-learning is especially encouraged in Australia, both to help students from non-English backgrounds keep in touch with their own cultures and to teach Australians languages that they may need for business. The most popular non-English language is Chinese, but Italian, Japanese, Korean, and Indonesian are also taught. In suburbs such as Redfern, Aboriginal pupils are taught their own languages.

Further education

More than a third of Australians go on to further education, which is funded by the federal (national) government. Sydney has five public universities. The oldest is the University of Sydney, founded in 1850. Specialist colleges of this university are scattered across the city. The **Conservatorium** of Music, for example, is in the Royal Botanic Gardens (see page 16). Other universities include the University of New South Wales, Macquarie University, and the University of Western Sydney, which has seven separate campuses.

The main campus ▲ of the University of Sydney, near the city center, contains many old stone buildings and grassy **quadrangles.**

OVERSEAS STUDENTS

Sydney universities educate Australians from a wide variety of **ethnic** backgrounds. Since the 1980s, overseas students have also been actively encouraged to enroll at the city's universities. Many thousands have done so. The vast majority of these students are from **Asia-Pacific countries** such as China and India.

INDUSTRY AND FINANCE

Sydney's first major industry was whaling, but the sale and export of wool and wheat soon became more important. In 1890 and again in the 1930s, economic **depression** hit the city. Since those difficult years, Sydney has steadily grown to become a major industrial and business center with links right across the world.

The skyscrapers of Sydney's **Central Business District** contain thousands of busy people hoping to make successful deals and large amounts of money.

Sydney's industries

Most of Sydney's workers have jobs in the health care and social services industries. Many others work in retail trade, professional, scientific and technical services, and manufacturing. Sydney's factories are more focused on high-tech manufacturing such as advanced electronics and biotechnology. The enormous appeal of the city also means that tourism is among Sydney's fastest-growing industries. In 2014-15, more than 32 million tourists visited the city.

Twin ports

Two container ports, in Sydney Harbor and Botany Bay, handle most of Australia's imports and exports. Coal, wool and beef are exported, as well as manufactured goods. Major imports are cars and **crude petroleum**. China buys more Australian exports than any other country, followed by Japan and South Korea.

Business and banking

Sydney's Central Business District (CBD) and its smaller equivalent in North Sydney make up the most important financial center in Australia. Smartly dressed men and women work in its skyscrapers for the country's leading businesses, banks and law firms from early in the morning until late at night. Nearly 60 banks, including the mighty Westpac Banking Corporation, have their headquarters in the city, as well as most of Australia's top 100 companies. The city is also the main base of the Reserve Bank of Australia, which issues the country's bank notes, and of the Australian Stock Exchange.

◄ Construction cranes loom above the harborside area of Bangaroo, one of several sites of new mixed-use development in and around Sydney to mix housing and businesses.

CRIME AND PUNISHMENT

Street and house burglary were common in early Sydney. By the late 19th century, gangs of thugs known as larrikins roamed the city, terrorizing its inhabitants. They committed many serious crimes, including murder. Bushrangers (highwaymen) such as Jack Donahoe and Mad-Dog Morgan lived on the outskirts of Sydney and made a living by stealing from the rich.

◀ Bushrangers lie in wait for a mail coach in the 19th century. Many of the first bushrangers were runaway convicts.

▼ Sydney is quite a safe city, where serious crimes are rare. Police officers like these are available to help anyone who needs them.

Sydney police

There are several separate police forces in Australia. The Australian Federal Police are based in the national capital, Canberra. They deal with major crime that crosses **state** boundaries, such as drug smuggling, counterterrorism, human trafficking, and cybercrime. New South Wales operates its own police force to deal with local crimes. In Sydney, both police officers wear a blue uniform with a hat, and are usually armed. They generally make foot patrols around the city. To move around more quickly they use either motorcycles or vans equipped with flashing lights.

Sydney's Justice and Police Museum is near the Rocks area of the city (see page 15), where many thugs used to lurk. Here you can examine photos and **plaster casts** of notorious Sydney criminals, as well as some of the terrifying weapons that they used. You can also see a restored **booking room** and magistrates' court, or even step into a gloomy prison cell.

Sydney Aborigines and their ▼ supporters march through the city to protest against the large number of Aborigine deaths in police custody.

Common crimes

The most common crime encountered by Australians and foreign residents alike in Sydney are assaults and breaking and entering. Pickpockets are active in areas such as Kings Cross and the central business district. Police advise people to leave their valuables at home or in their hotel. Possession of even small amounts of illegal substances can lead to jail. Murders in Sydney are rare—about one for every 100,000 Sydneysiders.

Organized crime

Organized gangs have operated in Sydney for years. They arrange crimes and run illegal businesses such as drug-dealing and gambling. As new communities arrived, new gangs emerge, including Chinese **Triads**. Organized crime groups have a presence in Sydney. They are mostly involved in drug trafficking, financial crime, or money laundering.

Aboriginal arrest

Aborigines are about 10 times more likely to be arrested and imprisoned than non-Aborigines. Aboriginal deaths in police custody are also a problem. In 1991 a **Royal Commission** report listed more than 300 ways to improve the situation and for a while things improved as the police attended programs to eliminate racist attitudes. However, since 2006 deaths in custody have risen each year.

GETTING AROUND

Sydney's location on two shores of a harbor, plus its huge network of suburbs, mean that a good transport system is vital. Early Sydneysiders traveled by horse-drawn carriage, tram or steam ferry. In the mid-19th century the railway arrived, and in the 20th century people began to use cars. Now there is a great variety of ways to get around.

▲ This is the famous Indian-Pacific train that carries passengers from Sydney to Perth in Western Australia in 72 hours.

Train travel

Rail travel within Sydney is provided by the Sydney Trains and NSW TrainLink system, which runs underground in the city center. The double-decker trains speed along six lines that extend far into the suburbs. A Light Rail line runs from the city to the west, and a second line links the center with eastern suburbs. Trains to other parts of Australia leave from the Central Railway Station.

UNDERGROUND

The extensive Sydney subway system might be getting even bigger in years to come. An expanding population and overcrowded roadways are sending officials scrambling for ways to move more people more quickly. The busy downtown system is going to expand to include suburban routes and connect with other rail systems.

On the bus

There are three main types of bus in Sydneys. Blue and white buses operate on a wide range of routes in the center of the city. Red Explorer buses make trips around 22 tourist sites, while double-decker Sydney and Bondi Explorers head for the beaches.

◀ To catch a water taxi, people simply raise an arm as though they are trying to stop a bus.

Ferries and water taxis

Traveling by water makes sense in a harborside city. Ferries travel from Circular Quay to more than 30 places, including Manly and Taronga Zoo. Passengers can travel on a standard ferry or a much quicker JetCat. People also hail water taxis, which take them wherever they want to go—at a price.

Traffic congestion ▶ is a very common sight nowadays on Sydney Harbor Bridge, especially in the early evening as people travel home from work.

Air travel

Sydney's airport, north of Botany Bay, is called Sydney Kingsford Smith Airport. It is the busiest in Australia for domestic and international flights. In 1994 a third runway was opened to cope with all the traffic. The airport is named after Sir Charles Kingsford Smith, a famous Australian airman of the 1920s and '30s.

Car culture

Most Sydneysiders learn to drive while they are teenagers and many families have two or more cars. As a result, Sydney has a serious traffic problem. Sydney Harbor Tunnel was opened in 1992 to ease pressure on Sydney Harbor Bridge. **Expressways** were built to improve traffic flow. But city authorities are constantly struggling to reduce traffic jams and ease air pollution.

ENTERTAINMENT

A magnificent arts center stands at Sydney's heart—the Opera House. But the city also has many other wonderful theaters, as well as hundreds of street entertainers. And Sydney is a great place to watch almost every kind of sport.

▲ An orchestra performs in the concert hall of the Sydney Opera House. The rings that hang above their heads improve the sound quality.

At the opera

Many people go to Sydney Opera House to see opera in the specially designed theater. There is much more on offer too. The Sydney Symphony Orchestra gives frequent performances in the 2,690-seat concert hall. The Drama Theater hosts the productions of the Sydney Theater Company, many by Australian writer David Williamson, while the smaller Playhouse often shows plays from abroad. The Australian Ballet and the Sydney Dance Company, a modern dance group, also perform in the Opera House. There are about 3,000 shows of all sorts in the complex every year.

Theater time

Sydney's oldest theater is the Theatre Royal. It was founded in 1833 by Barnett Levey, 'the father of Australian theatre', and is still open. The richly decorated State Theater, with its marble staircase, glittering chandeliers and Wurlitzer organ, opened in 1929 as a grand picture palace (cinema). Now it shows films throughout the year and hosts the Sydney Film Festival in June. It also has live entertainment, particularly musicals.

▼ Film-lovers can watch the stars on Darling Harbor's IMAX cinema, the world's largest!

MODERN MUSIC

People who prefer rock and pop to classical music have plenty of choice in Sydney. A variety of famous bands played at Qantas Credit Union Arena, but it is scheduled to be replaced in late 2016 by a larger venue. Another place to see the stars is the State Theatre, while new bands look for their big break at small clubs, including many local pubs.

▲Large crowds attend both one-day contests and Test Matches lasting up to five days at Sydney Cricket Ground.

Sports scene

Sydneysiders love to play all kinds of sport. They also have many opportunities to watch the professionals. International cricket matches are held at Sydney Cricket Ground. **Australian Rules Football** is also played here, and rugby league at the nearby Allianz Stadium is very popular. Horse racing is a passion for many in Sydney. Randwick is the most famous of the city's four racecourses and over 50 meetings a year are held there.

MUSEUMS AND ART GALLERIES

Sydney is packed with museums, including one devoted to the city itself. There are plenty of galleries, too, where art-lovers can spend hours gazing at everything from Aboriginal **acrylics** to Picassos.

This sculpture, *Edge of the Trees*, stands outside the Museum of Sydney. Two artists, one of them Aborigine, made it together.

The Museum of Sydney

The Museum of Sydney stands on the site of the old Government House, where New South Wales' first eight governors lived. Its exhibits tell the story of the city from 1788 to 1850, from the point of view of both Eora Aborigines and European settlers. Special features include Gadigal Place gallery, where the story of the Gadigal clan, original inhabitants of the area now known as Sydney, is told.

The Australian Museum

This natural history museum focuses on the wildlife of Australia and the Pacific region, whether extinct or still living. It houses displays of all sorts of creatures, as well as many skeletons, including Eric the **plesiosaur** and ten other complete skeletons. The museum also has Aboriginal and Torres Straits collections that contain rare ceremonial and everyday objects.

ELIZABETH BAY HOUSE

The beautiful Elizabeth Bay House, completed in 1838, stands in the suburb of Kings Cross. The architect was John Verge, who designed the building for Alexander Macleay, then the Colonial Secretary of New South Wales. Macleay spent so much money on his mansion that he went bankrupt and had to move out. In 1977 the house became a museum, and was refurnished. Visitors can explore the upstairs rooms and the cellars.

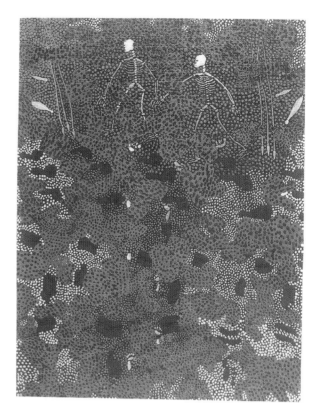

The Powerhouse Museum

The award-winning Powerhouse Museum, part of the Museum of Applied Arts and Sciences, is the largest in Australia. The main themes of the museum are science and technology. Other subjects, including Australian life, are also covered in its five areas. Among the many exhibits are a steam engine and a flying boat suspended from the ceiling. There are also hands-on displays that make science fun.

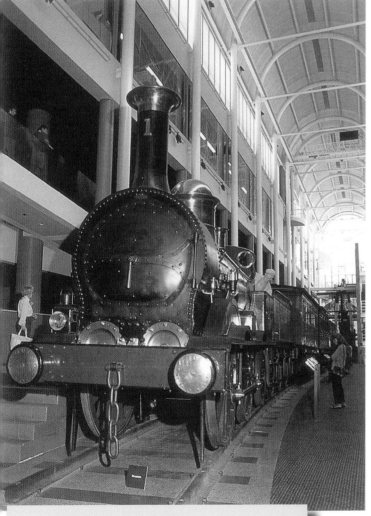

The Powerhouse Museum contains this ▲ wonderful steam train. It was the first ever to run in New South Wales.

Art galleries

The Art Gallery of New South Wales displays paintings by Australian artists such as Sidney Nolan, and a few works by major European names such as Picasso. The Yiribana Gallery, which opened within the main gallery in 1994, contains more than 2,000 examples of Aboriginal and Torres Strait Islander art (from the Torres Strait, off the coast of Northeast Australia). These works include sculptures and bark paintings. The gallery also has Asian art and stunning photographs.

Harborside art

The Museum of Contemporary Art was opened on the harborside in 1991. It was funded with money left by an Australian art collector called John Wardell Power, who died in 1943. Australia's best collection of modern art, including works by Andy Warhol and Roy Lichtenstein, is displayed there.

SHOPS AND MARKETS

People can buy almost anything in the shops and markets of modern Sydney, from clothes by top international designers to Australian art. There is a huge array of goods on offer, and more tourists shop in the city than go to the Sydney Opera House.

Shopping centers

The Queen Victoria Building is one of the oldest shopping centers in Sydney. It was built in 1898 as a market, then served as a library, a warehouse and offices before falling into disrepair. In the 1980s it was returned to its former glory. Now there are over 200 shops and restaurants under its copper domes. Its Victorian windows, castiron staircase and lift have all been restored. The nearby Skygarden is a modern shopping precinct. It sells expensive designer goods and has a cafe and restaurant under its glass roof.

▲ Sydney's Strand Arcade is a 19th-century shopping complex that has been restored for modern use. It was built in 1892.

▲ The huge, glittering perfume department at David Jones, one of the city's leading stores.

Department stores

Sydney has two main department stores: Meyer and David Jones. The more upscale retailer is David Jones, which calls itself "the most beautiful store in the world." It opened in the mid-19th century on one site, but now fills two separate buildings. The Elizabeth Street branch is the place to buy expensive clothes, perfume, and cosmetics. It is also known for its beautiful window displays at Christmas and flower displays in the spring. The Market Street branch's main attraction is its splendid food hall.

Sydney Fish Market

Sydney Fish Market attracts both expert fishmongers and ordinary seafood-lovers. Early in the day, professionals bid for the amazing range of marine and freshwater creatures on offer. Some are then sold in market shops. Blue swimmer crabs, Sydney Harbor prawns, and **barramundi** are just a few of the edible delights that tempt the crowds.

Hundreds of types of fish ▲ are on sale at the Sydney Fish Market. Here, a trader prepares slices of raw tuna.

General markets

There are many general markets in Sydney, each with its own character. Among the best is the Paddington Market, which takes place every Saturday. Goods for sale include fashionable clothes, pottery, and silver jewelry. Paddy's Market at Haymarket is held in a covered site near Darling Harbor. It opened in 1869, making it the city's oldest market. With 1,000 stalls, it is also the largest. Food, flowers, clothes, electrical goods, even pets can be bought under its vast roof.

AUSTRALIANA

Australiana—typically Australian goods—are among the most commonly purchased items in Sydney shops. They include opals, kangaroo-skin rugs, macadamia nuts, and Aboriginal arts and crafts like this sculpture (right). Traditional clothing is popular, too. Shops stock the felt hats, oilskin coats, and **moleskin** trousers worn by rugged Australian farmers.

FOOD AND DRINK

At the time when most people in Sydney were British or Irish, the food was plain and heavy—a typical meal was meat pie, tomato sauce, and mashed potato. Immigrants from China, Italy, Greece, and elsewhere have transformed eating and drinking in the city. Now, at home and in restaurants, a huge range of delicious dishes is prepared.

▲ Sydnesiders enjoy barbecues in their garden, on beaches, or in the city's parks.

BUSH TUCKER

Foods traditionally eaten by Aborigines include crocodiles, wallabies, and **witchetty grubs**, as well as a variety of rainforest fruits (above). Now this food, sometimes known as bush tucker, is making its way into Sydney restaurants. Until 2007, Edna's Table served these foods in a room decorated with Aboriginal art. Today, Edna's operates food trucks around the city.

Home cooking

Plenty of locally produced fresh food is available in Sydney. There is fish and shellfish, as well as lamb and other meats from nearby farms. Fruits, vegetables and cheeses from elsewhere in Australia are on offer, as well as imported foods. The range is increasing. Before 1993, for example, it was illegal to eat kangaroo, but now it often appears on meat counters. Sydneysiders cook everything from roast joints with potatoes to pizzas and Thai curries. They often barbecue steaks, chicken, sausages, prawns, and octopus.

Café society

Italian immigrants set up the first real cafés in Sydney and now there are hundreds, especially in the inner suburb of Darlinghurst. The most famous is the Italian-themed Bar Coluzzi, which serves a specially blended coffee and delicious snacks. The city's best-loved cafe is a more down-to-earth establishment. Harry's Café de Wheels started as nothing more than a caravan in Woolloomooloo, near the Botanic Gardens. It was set up in 1945 to sell old-style Australian food and still does today, and has added many other locations. One of its most popular dishes is the Pie Floater—meat pie drifting on a sea of pea soup.

▲ One of the most popular eating spots in Sydney is anywhere with a harbor view. Restaurants can be found at many locations harborside.

▲ Hungry Sydneysiders cluster around Harry's Cafe de Wheels. Many people come here after a night on the town.

Restaurant meals

Today, there are about 6,000 restaurants in Sydney. Some of the best specialize in seafood. Doyles in Watsons Bay was among the first to begin this trend, in 1885. It sells freshly cooked fish and chips that customers can eat while gazing out over the harbor. Rockpool in the Rocks is the place for gourmet dishes. There, people can eat fish such as fresh tuna cooked with Asian herbs and spices. This mixed style of cooking is known as Modern Australian.

SPECIAL EVENTS

There are special activities to enjoy during every one of Sydney's seasons, from high summer to the depths of winter.

Summer celebrations

The three-week-long Sydney Festival starts the year with a bang. Every January, when the weather is hottest, there are open-air events across the city. The climax is on 26 January, Australia Day. People commemorate the arrival of Captain Phillip (see pages 8-9) and the birth of Sydney with celebrations including a concert in The Domain and fireworks in Darling Harbor. Chinatown is extra lively in late January or early February, at Chinese New Year. Lion dancers wear colourful costumes, while firecrackers explode around them.

▼ Sydneysiders on Australia Day, dressed in 18th-century naval uniforms, re-enact the arrival of Captain Arthur Phillip.

Large, colorful kites soar above ▼ Bondi Beach during September's Festival of the Winds.

Autumn events

There are two spectacular street events in March. On the first Saturday of the month, Sydney's Gay and Lesbian **Mardi Gras** Parade takes place. About 400,000 gay people live in the city and many more arrive from all over the world to join them in this extravagant carnival. On St. Patrick's Day (17 March), the city's Irish population celebrates with another massive street parade that winds slowly through the city.

Winter and spring

The Film Festival in June is a major event in the Sydney winter. But people who prefer keeping fit to sitting in a cinema have plenty to keep them busy as well. Almost anyone with enough enthusiasm can run the 8.6-mile (14-km) City to Surf Race from Hyde Park to Bondi Beach. The Blackmores Sydney Running Festival in August includes the Sydney Marathon for top runners, plus other events for amateurs and families. In September, Bondi Beach hosts the Festival of the Winds, during which people fly their kites to create a sensational display.

◄ Sydneysiders have a chance to meet the farmers of New South Wales at the Royal Easter Show. They can watch show-jumping and prize cattle or admire the giant pumpkins and vegetables.

CHRISTMAS AND NEW YEAR

Sydney hosts two major open-air events over Christmas. On Christmas Day thousands of people, usually tourists, go to Bondi Beach for a festive picnic. On Boxing Day (December 26), crowds gather in Sydney Harbor to watch the start of the Sydney to Hobart Yacht Race (below), a voyage to the capital of Tasmania. New Year's Eve is the occasion for another celebration. Parties go on all night and dazzling firework displays light up the sky.

CITY CHARACTERS

Since Sydney was founded, it has been home to an array of colorful characters. Many have made a lasting mark on its history.

Francis Greenway

Francis Greenway worked as an architect in Bristol. He was sentenced to death for forging a contract, but was then transported to the Sydney **penal colony**. Two years after his arrival he became a government architect. By 1822 he had designed 40 buildings, including St. James' Church and Hyde Park Barracks. Later the British government fired him for extravagance.

After losing his job, Francis Greenway ▲ soon lost all his money too. He died penniless in 1837. His grave is unmarked.

Joan Sutherland

Opera singer Joan Sutherland was born in Sydney in 1926 and first appeared on stage there in 1951. She went to London to study at the Royal College of Music and to sing at the Royal Opera House. Sutherland has performed at opera houses around the world, including the Metropolitan in New York. Her beautiful soprano voice won her great praise. She retired in 1990.

◄ Joan Sutherland, dressed for a major operatic role. She often sang Italian operas by composers such as Vincenzo Bellini.

▼ Patrick White's novels include Vbss (1957). It is based on the true story of Ludwig Leichhardt, a man who explored the Australian deserts.

Patrick White

The writer Patrick White was born to Australian parents in London in 1912. He grew up in both Australia and England, but in 1948 settled in Sydney and became a full-time author. The themes of his work include the trials of Australia's early settlers and the shallowness of Sydneysiders. In 1973 White won the Nobel Prize for Literature.

Pat O'Shane

Pat O'Shane was born in the **state** of Queensland, north of New South Wales, but Sydney has long been her home. She was the first Aborigine to qualify as a lawyer and in 1976 became a barrister. Ten years later she was also made a magistrate. In the 1980s O'Shane ran the Aboriginal Affairs Department of the New South Wales government.

SYDNEY STARS

Many Hollywood stars have links with Sydney. Paul Hogan grew up in the city and worked on Sydney Harbor Bridge. He entered a television talent contest and never looked back. The film *Crocodile Dundee* brought him world fame. Mel Gibson is Australian, although he was born in the USA, and gained fame and Oscars for *Braveheart*, among others. Hugh Jackman (right) is in the X-Men films and stars on Broadway. Iggy Azalea has become an international pop singing star.

SYDNEY'S FUTURE

The future of Sydney probably will be determined by how it deals with an ever-changing population, as it becomes a more and more international city each year. Other everyday changes are also taking place that will have an impact on Sydney life.

▼ Many old buildings are being renovated. This office block now houses the Museum of Contemporary Art.

People power

Sydney's population mix is constantly altering. In recent years, the largest number of new Sydneysiders has come from countries such as Vietnam, Indonesia, Malaysia, and the Philippines. The Chinese community has made Chinese the second most widely spoken language in the city. People from Sydney's many cultures now influence all areas of life, particularly trade, education, and politics, and they are gradually changing the nature of the city.

Building the future

Sydney is a city of suburbs. But developers are increasingly creating new homes in converted city-center tower blocks and warehouses. They are renovating run-down inner suburbs such as Surry Hills to attract people there. This policy can bring life and money to dying areas, but it can also force the original residents to leave. Many of the new buildings are in what some are calling the "Sydney Style," reflecting the curves of the famous Opera House and the shoreline of the Harbor.

The British Connection

In 1999 Australians voted agasint having their country split fully from Great Britain. Australia remains independent, but the British monarch is still officially Australia's head of state. However, as closely allied as Australia is with Great Britain, its relations with its Asian neighbors—China, Indonesia, India, and others—will continue to grow in importance.

SYDNEY TOMORROW

Sydney's leaders, in some cases building on the success of the 2000 Summer Olympics in the region, have been moving toward big plans for this growing city, expected to reach 5 million people in the next decade. Major highway, hospital, and transportation projects are planned for almost every area of the city. Getting people to and from the suburbs will be an increasingly big problem that organizers and government are trying to plan for. Sections of the harborside will be developed into new areas for housing, shops, and tourism. A city that started as a home for convicts has become a world-class site.

Ozzie! Ozzie! Ozzie!

In 2015, Australia and New Zealand jointly hosted the ICC Cricket World Cup. More than a billion people tuned in to the final, played in Melbourne. Sydney was the scene of tremendous parties after Australia captured the Cup with a dramatic win over New Zealand. Cricket remains a popular sport in Australia.

Australians from coast to coast celebrated the 2015 ▲ Cricket World Cup champions of their hometown heroes.

TIMELINE

This timeline shows some of the most important dates in Sydney's history.

PRE-18TH CENTURY

c.40,000 years ago

*Aborigines reach Australia from
Southeast Asia*

c.20,000 years ago

Aborigines settle in Sydney Harbor area

18TH CENTURY

1770

*Captain James Cook lands in Botany Bay,
claims Australia's east coast for Britain and
names it New South Wales*

1786

*British government decides to set up
a penal colony in Botany Bay*

1787

*First Fleet, led by Captain Arthur Phillip,
sets sail from Britain*

1788

*First Fleet arrives in Sydney and Captain
Phillip founds settlement*

1790

Second Fleet arrives in Sydney

19TH CENTURY

1810-1821

*Lachlan Macquarie is Governor of
New South Wales*

1813

Explorers cross Blue Mountains west of Sydney

1814

Francis Greenway arrives in Sydney

1816

Cadman's Cottage completed

1819

Hyde Park Barracks completed

1820

St. James' Church completed

1833

Theatre Royal, Sydney's first theatre, opens

1838

Elizabeth Bay House completed

1840

*British government stops sending criminals
to New South Wales*

1842

Sydney becomes a city

1850

Sydney University founded

1851

*Gold discovered west of Blue Mountains;
gold rush begins*

1855

Parliament set up in Sydney

1856

*Sydney becomes capital of New South
Wales colony*

Royal Botanic Gardens founded

1858

Sydney Observatory built

1869

Paddy's Market opens

1885

Doyles restaurant opens in Watsons Bay

1887

Customs House built

1888

Sydney celebrates its centenary

1890

Economic depression hits Sydney

1892

Strand Arcade opens

1898

Queen Victoria Building opens

20TH CENTURY

1900

112 people die following an outbreak of plague

1901

Australia formed and Sydney becomes capital of New South Wales state

1914-18

Many Sydneysiders fight in the First World War, particularly at Gallipoli (1915-16)

1916

Taronga Zoo opens

1929

State Theatre opens

1930s

Economic depression hits Sydney

1932

Sydney Harbor Bridge opens

1939-45

Many Sydney siders fight in the Second World War

1942

Japanese submarines sail into Sydney harbor and are sunk

1947

Post-war immigration begins

1960s

Asian immigrants begin to arrive in Australia

1973

Sydney Opera House opens

1989

Australian government publishes its National Agenda for a Multicultural Australia

1991

Royal Commission report on police treatment of Aborigines published Museum of Contemporary Art opens

1992

Sydney Harbor Tunnel opens

1993

It becomes legal to eat kangaroo meat in Australia

1999

Australians vote whether Australia should become a republic; the vote fails

21ST CENTURY

2000

Sydney hosted the Olympic and Paralympic Games

2001

Australia celebrated its 200th birthday

2003

Drought and wildfires ravage Australia

2004

Riots strike Sydney after the death of an Aboriginal boy in police custody

2008

Quentin Bryce becomes Australia's first female governor-general

2011

Queensland floods devastate the area

2014

Australia leads the way for the search for a missing Malaysian Airlines jet

GLOSSARY

acrylic   A work of art created with acrylic paints made from a chemical called acrylic acid. Acrylic paints are used by many modern Aboriginal artists.

Anglican   Belonging to the Church of England or an associated church.

Asia-Pacific countries   Asian countries that lie in or border the Pacific Ocean, particularly its southern section. They include Japan, Indonesia, and Malaysia.

Australian Rules Football   A type of football that is a mixture of rugby, Gaelic (Irish) football, and ordinary football. Teams have 18 players each. They play with an oval ball on an oval field.

barramundi   A type of Australian freshwater fish with a long, scaly body and large, wide fins.

Central Business District   The central area of a city where the major businesses are based. Every Australian city has a Central Business District (CBD).

Conservatorium   The Australian word for an advanced school or college of music. The American term is usually *conservatory*.

container ships   Large ships that carry cargo packed in standard-sized containers.

crude petroleum   Oil that has not yet been refined to make gasoline or paraffin, but remains in its natural state.

depression (economic)   A time of low business growth, high unemployment, and falling prices.

expressway   A highway designed to carry fast traffic through a city or town.

extended family   A family that contains not only parents and their children but also grandparents, aunts, uncles, etc.

federation   A country or other political unit in which power is shared between several regional governments and a single national government.

gable   A triangular section of an outside house wall between the sloping ends of an overhanging roof.

Governor-General   The high-ranking official whose job it is to represent the British king or queen in Australia.

Greenwich Mean Time   The time in Greenwich, England, which stands on the zero line of longitude. It is used as a base for calculating the time in the rest of the world.

head of state   The official head of a country. Many heads of state, including the British queen, do not have much real political power.

herbarium   A collection of dried plants. The National Herbarium of New South Wales is also a center for the study of Australian plants.

kookaburra   A type of grey Australian kingfisher that lives in trees. It is famous for its strange call that sounds rather like laughter. Another name for this bird is "laughing jackass."

Mardi Gras   The French term for Fat Tuesday, and the name given to a festival celebrated in some countries on or around that day. Fat Tuesday occurs just before Lent, a period of 40 days in which many Christians used to fast or give up certain foods. On Shrove Tuesday they ate rich foods and had fun before the fasting began. Now most people join in the celebrations without fasting afterwards.

moleskin   A type of strong cotton fabric.

Paralympic Games   A major games and athletics meeting at which disabled people compete.

pavilion   A decorative building that provides shelter but is usually open to the outside.

penal colony   A place where criminals are sent to be punished.

plaster casts   Molds made from plaster of Paris, a type of white powder that sets solid.

plesiosaur   A type of reptile that lived in the sea millions of years ago. Plesiosaurs had long necks and paddle-like limbs. They could grow to a length of 40 feet.

prospectors   People who search for gold and other precious metals in the ground, rivers etc.

quadrangle   A four-sided, usually rectangular courtyard surrounded by buildings.

regatta   A series of yacht and other boat races.

republican   A person who believes that countries should be governed only by elected rulers and should not have kings or queens.

reservation   a tract of public land set aside (as for use by American Indians or, this case, Aborigines).

Royal Commission   A group of people selected by the government to enquire into a serious issue and to work out a plan of action. It is called a 'Royal' Commission as Queen Elizabeth II is the Australian head of state.

state   A country or other political unit that governs itself and makes its own laws. Australia is divided into six states. One of these is New South Wales, and Sydney is its capital.

witchetty grubs   The caterpillars of an Australian moth. Aborigines eat the grubs both cooked and raw.

World War I   A major war that lasted from 1914 to 1918 and involved many countries. Australians fought alongside the British, French, Russians (until 1917), and Americans (from 1917), to defeat Germany, Austria-Hungary and their allies.

World War II (WWII)   A major war that lasted from 1939 to 1945 and involved many countries. Australians joined with the British, French, Russians, and Americans (from 1941), to defeat Germany, Italy and their allies.

INDEX